Fall
2011

CONVERSATION

Conversation

THEODORE ZELDIN

Illustrated by the author

HiddenSpring

Designed and typeset in Trinité at
Libanus Press, Marlborough, Wiltshire

Published in Great Britain in 1998 by
The Harvill Press
2 Aztec Row, Berners Road
London N1 0PW

www.harvill-press.com

Library of Congress Cataloging-in-Publication Data

Zeldin, Theodore, 1933-
Conversation / Theodore Zeldin.
p. cm.
ISBN 1-58768-000-9 (alk. paper)
1. Conversation. 2. Oral communication. I. Title.

P95.45 .Z45 2000
302.3'46–dc21   00-038857

Published in North America by
HiddenSpring
an imprint of Paulist Press
997 Macarthur Boulevard
Mahwah, New Jersey 07430

www.hiddenspringbooks.com

Printed and bound in Mexico

Contents

The Pictures

Conversation is, among other things, a mind-reading game and a puzzle. We constantly have to guess why others say what they do. We can never be sure when words will dance with each other, opinions caress, imaginations undress, topics open. But we can become more agile if we wish.

Like love, conversation can be stimulated by the play of appearances. So I have sprinkled my text with some pictorial equivalents of aphrodisiacs. I hope that these pictures, by suggesting different ideas to those who look at them, may stimulate discussion about the different directions our imaginations like to travel. Even if aphrodisiacs don't work, at least they give a glimpse of the strange antics we play in our heads.

I have placed at the end of the book thirty-six topics of conversation, each provoked by one of these pictures. They are all questions about conversation. Just as lovers deepen and define their love by talking endlessly about love, so those who are hungry for more satisfying conversation need to talk about conversation. There is a lot of poetry about love, but virtually none about talk. We have to invent, however humbly, our substitute for it.

First words

1

*How every new era changes
the subject of conversation*

"It's good to talk," says British Telecom's advertisement. But of course that's only half the truth. Nobody could say simply, "It's good to eat," without adding that many of the things we like to eat do us no good at all. If we used diet books for our conversations, as much as for our meals, they would warn us off many different kinds of talk, and they would not find it easy to say where we could go to taste the *haute cuisine* of conversation.

"It's good to talk" was the slogan of the twentieth century, which put its faith in self-expression, sharing information and trying to be understood. But talking does not necessarily change one's own or other people's feelings or ideas. I believe

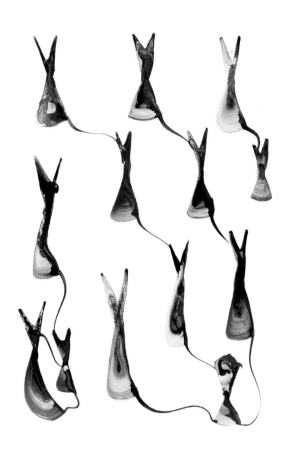

Copycats

the twenty-first century needs a new ambition, to develop not talk but conversation, which does change people. Real conversation catches fire. It involves more than sending and receiving information.

There have been thousands of books purporting to be about conversation, with instructions on how to flatter or deceive, or be seductive, or sound posh, or how to cope with people like Clark Gable, who – according to Ava Gardner – was "the sort of man that if you said 'Hello Clark, how are you?', he'd be kinda stuck for an answer." But I'm not going to offer you yet another collection of recipes, guaranteed to produce a style of talk you can show off to your friends. The kind of conversation I'm interested in is one which you start with a willingness to emerge a slightly different person. It is always an experiment, whose results are never guaranteed. It involves risk. It's an adventure in which we agree to cook the world together and make it taste less bitter.

Everything I'm going to say to you is the child of a conversation. My last book was the child of conversations I had with women from 18 countries, about what mattered most to them, their desires and fears. That led me to search for the conversations of women and men in the past as well, in all civilizations, on their desires and fears. Since then I have been having conversations with people about the way they conduct their conversations. I have read as much about conversation as I could, which meant having conversations with authors I met only on paper. I then thought about all this, which was a conversation with myself. I discussed the result with my wife, Deirdre Wilson, who has spent many years investigating what happens in people's minds when they communicate; we disagreed and argued and gave each other ideas we had not had before.

That is the aspect of conversation that particularly excites me: how conversation changes the way you see the world, and even changes the world. I want to discuss how this happens.

But how can conversations make so much difference? They can't if you believe that the world is ruled by over-powering economic and political forces, that conflict is the essence of life, that humans are basically animals and that history is just a long struggle for survival and domination. If that's true, you can't change much. All you can do is have conversations which distract or amuse you. But I see the world differently, as made of individuals searching for a partner, for a lover, for a guru, for God. The most important, life-changing events are the meetings of these individuals. Some people get disappointed, give up searching and become cynics. But some keep on searching for new meetings.

The gate between the public and the private

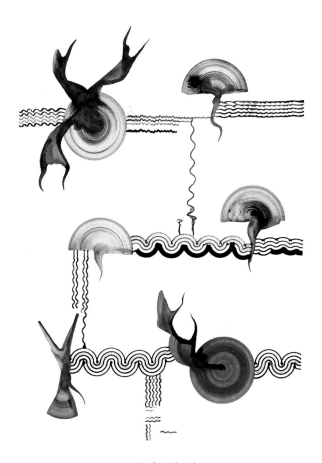

Emotional wavelengths

Humans have already changed the world several times by changing the way they have had conversations. There have been conversational revolutions which have been as important as wars and riots and famine. When problems have appeared insoluble, when life has seemed to be meaningless, when governments have been powerless, people have sometimes found a way out by changing the subject of their conversation, or the way they talked, or the persons they talked to. In the past that gave us the Renaissance, the Enlightenment, modernity and postmodernity. Now it's time for the New Conversation.

In the past, most people have been too frightened to talk much, publicly and even privately. It has been too dangerous or embarrassing or painful. There are still places where it is dangerous to speak. The powerful have always known that they are threatened by conversation. For most of history, the world has been governed by the conversation of intimidation or evasion. We cannot abolish timidity altogether, but we can redirect fears, so that they stimulate generosity rather than paralysis.

At times, when people have dared to speak, they have treated words as having almost divine status, to be respected and polished and adorned. That has produced some wonderful music. But it has also led some people to discover how to exploit words. They have tried to get their way by using rhetoric, packaging what they had to say to make it look more attractive, with flowery language – metaphors, alliteration, repetition, irony and paradox. The packaging could become more influential than what was said.

The poets Wordsworth and Samuel Rogers remembered once visiting Coleridge, one of the greatest exponents of rhetoric, who talked to them for two hours without giving them the chance to say a word. This is what Rogers reports: "When we left the house, we walked for some time without speaking.

'What a wonderful man he is!' exclaimed Wordsworth.

'Wonderful indeed,' said I.

'What depth of thought, what richness of expression,' continued Wordsworth.

'There is nothing like him that I ever heard,' rejoined I. Another pause.

'Pray,' enquired Wordsworth. 'Did you precisely understand what he said about the Kantian philosophy?'

'Not precisely.'

'Or about the plurality of worlds?'

'I can't say I did. In fact, if the truth must out, I did not understand a syllable from one end of his monologue to the other.'

A cruel word

The wasted meeting

'No more,' said Wordsworth, 'did I.'"

Rhetoric made speech persuasive. It was sometimes used as a bag of tricks which got others to agree and to swoon and to admire, whatever you said. You won power by using words. It became a diet rather like the old-fashioned cooking which heaped sauce and spice on food, concealing what was underneath. People enjoyed it because they enjoyed being charmed, and they became the slaves of what they thought was beauty. Winning an argument became a substitute for discovering the truth. Forcing others to agree became the source of self-esteem. Rhetoric became a weapon of war, subjugating millions.

But there are more interesting things in life than polishing one's armor. People began rejecting this style of speaking, for two quite different reasons. It seemed useless as a tool for accurate scientific description, a positive hindrance by distracting with analogies and poetic comparisons. The growth of interest in science led to a change of style. Speaking and writing clearly, without frills, forced people to develop a more scientific attitude, to abandon magic and superstition. And also people began to criticize rhetoric as anti-democratic: snobbish, deliberately obscure, repressive of real feelings. They equated it with the cult of the genteel, the desire to be superior. Plain talk triumphed in the United

States in the nineteenth century, forcing the pretentious to stop tyrannizing others with their etiquette or affectation. But plain talk sometimes degenerated into a rejection of standards and an admiration for the speech of the uneducated. It became even more obscure than rhetoric. In the same way, scientific clarity was carried so far that it became jargon, comprehensible only to the initiated. Scientific talk was the equivalent of health food. Plain talk was the equivalent of fast food.

The ideals of conversation remained masculine, until women changed the subject. They showed that talking about the emotions could not only improve the way the sexes treated each other, but also diminish brutality and aggressiveness in general. This new conversation was like vegetarian cooking: it convinced only a minority. Most men continued to prefer the bawdiness, slapstick, shop talk or academic disputation which they could indulge in when women were not present.

In the twentieth century, a great attempt was made to change the subject of conversation again by eliminating racist and sexist talk. This has been only partially successful, but it has had a great influence on the way people behave toward each other. Of course, constraints on speech can turn into "political correctness" and a repression of a new kind. Every slimming diet has its dangers.

Even witty conversation. Wit, which punctures the balloons of pompous talk, enables the disadvantaged to cut the powerful down to size. For example, Charles Lamb turned his stutter to good account by little interruptions, by his refusal to take life too seriously. When a doctor recommended a walk every day on an empty stomach, Lamb interrupted, "Whose stomach?" Wit has been humanity's liberator against the boredom that most conversation has induced, humanity's protector against speakers who get drunk on their own verbosity. But wit can be like *nouvelle cuisine*. It can leave you dazzled but hungry. It may sharpen the mind, but on its own it contains no nourishment.

Hollywood's leading expert on conversation, Lillian Glass, who teaches the stars how to talk, revealing her secrets in a book, writes: "As a communications specialist, I believe that all communication problems can be solved." British Telecom, having told us that "It's good to talk", has sent every household in the country a booklet spelling out how to make talk comprehensible and sensitive, emphasizing clarity above all. But we need more than a sort of AAA repairman mending conversations enough to stop them breaking down again. We have to decide for ourselves where to drive, what to use our powers of conversation for.

Conversation is not just about conveying information or sharing emotions, nor just a way of putting ideas into people's heads. The experts can help you understand the mechanisms. But to try to learn to converse better by applying some technique, on the model of Masters and Johnson's instructions on how to be good at sex, won't get you very far.

Conversation is a meeting of minds with different memories and habits. When minds meet, they don't just exchange facts: they transform them, reshape them, draw different implications from them, engage in new trains of thought. Conversation doesn't just reshuffle the cards: it creates new cards. That's the part that interests me. That's where I find the excitement. It's like a spark that two minds create. And what I really care about is what new conversational banquets one can create from those sparks.

For example: many people do work that's boring, or doesn't make them more interesting as individuals. I want to show how a new conversation could change that. Much of the conversation in our private life does nothing to make us more generous. Is there a new language of love – beyond chatting up – to be learned, which will help us treat one another with more respect? Much of technology has added stress and confusion to our lives. Can a new type of conversation give us instead the courage to realize that we can make our own choices? Most religions have difficulty in talking to one another. Is there a way that they can at last learn to converse with sympathy? I think all that is possible, and I will explain how in our next conversation, which is unfortunately only a semi-conversation. I regret that I can't hear what you're saying or thinking or screaming in protest while I talk. I wish I could.

But let me try and answer an objection that might occur to you. Surely not everybody has the gift of being able to converse: what about all those who are naturally quiet, or introverted, and what about the enormous numbers who are shy? What part can they expect to play, if conversation were to become the most important kind of interaction, and the main agent of change?

I don't think you have to be talkative to converse, or even to have a quick mind. Pauses in conversation do no harm. One of the most memorable conversationalists in history, the French diplomat Talleyrand, who suffered from a lonely upbringing and a physical handicap, would often sit through a party without saying a word, but then suddenly come out with a sentence which people said was the sort they never forgot. What matters is whether you are willing to think for yourself, and to say what you think. Many people are not, either because they've been told too often that they are just ordinary people and they assume they have nothing of importance to say, or because they have received too many knocks from life.

My answer is that throughout history, ordinary people have suddenly come out with the most amazing statements, when they find the courage. What matters most is courage. The most rewarding discovery I have made in my study of history has been about the way people who do not think of themselves as brave forget their reticence, their hesitations, and do brave things. Mice, more often than we realize, have been able to move mountains. And since so many of those who have power and authority are failing to move the mountains on our behalf, let us see what we can do ourselves, using our own brains and our own tongues.

2

Why the conversation of love is moving in a new direction

They forgot in the news this morning to tell us how many relationships, engagements and affairs were broken off yesterday. And how many of these collapsed because the woman complained that the man didn't talk to her enough. Stanford University has reported that 50% of American men now feel nervous in the company of women and that flirting is a dying art, because men are wary of accusations of harassment. Research in England claims that the same is happening there. What's the point of yearning for long conversations when yet more studies show that "You can tell in the first four minutes whether a person is going to be your friend, lover, or merely an acquaintance"?

In the course of history, humans have invented several

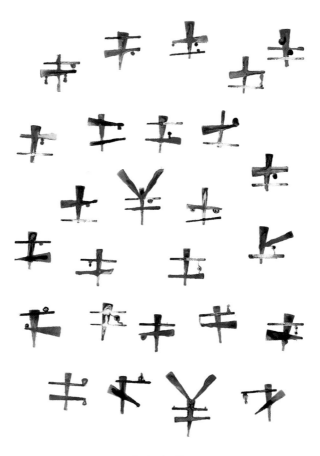

The signals of love

kinds of loving conversations, each of which has given a different shape to our relationships. But they are like languages whose vocabulary is inadequate. We have to invent a new kind of love talk to suit our aspirations today.

The original way to chat up a woman was to woo her. To woo originally meant to show off your strength and wealth, to impress, to conquer. Very little talking was needed. As a Chinese saying put it: "We communicate by eating together". Women, for their part, used to rely on magic, not conversation, to attract men, and then to stop them going off with other women.

In the fifteenth century a new word came into vogue: "to court". Courtiers, of both sexes, forced to spend long hours in each other's company, developed a sort of game. Wooing was what men did to women. Courting was a shared activity. The central subject of the conversation of courtship was loyalty, and whether the promise of loyalty would be kept. But male courtiers said: "It is a courtier's profession to court every dame, but to be constant to none." When this game was played brilliantly, it meant exciting conversation about what love and loyalty meant, what the ideals of life should be, a game played with exquisite politeness. When the game was played by wolves bent on social advancement, it meant lying and cheating.

First impressions

A third language, civil conversation, was popularized by an Italian called Guazzo, whose book, first published in 1574, was translated almost immediately into English and other languages. Guazzo focused on urbanity, the art of living together with decency, without quarrels or violence. He advised honesty and kindness, attentiveness to a woman's feelings, winning her love by discovering her good qualities, using words not force. Guazzo insisted, "A man cannot be a right man without conversation." But he was read by only a small elite (which included George Washington). The world continued to admire violence, so he could not become the Dr Spock of companionate marriage.

A fourth language is the romantic one, propagated by poets and novelists. At first it was the language of revolution, by lovers against their parents, by women against control of their affections. It exalted sex as the embodiment of love. Its principal theme was passion. But it was based on two ultimately unacceptable premises: on men idealizing their partner so that they didn't need to know her properly. And on treating love as a thunderbolt from heaven, uncontrollable, to which one had to be a willing victim. It assumed that suffering was an essential ingredient of love, and neuroticism a frequent consequence. It even, as Boswell put it, made men "pretend to feel every species of anguish

He loves me, he loves me not

experienced by illustrious prototypes." Life imitated novels and poetry, which wrote your lines for you.

But of course not everyone succeeded in talking like a courtier or a poet. Even though many people memorized the jokes and compliments collected in etiquette books, many conversations, as Swift observed, still had a tendency to die quickly, "like fire without fuel". Many men didn't seem to want to hear what women had to say, and found nothing wrong with Jane Austen's sad comment, "Imbecility in females is a great enhancer of their personal charms." Mrs Trollope, visiting America in the 1830s, complained that, "The two sexes hardly mix without great restraint or ennui." A century later, Olive Heseltine wrote, "To nearly all women . . . talk with the male youth of England is neither interesting nor intelligible."

The tragedy of the twentieth century was that it did not develop models for another kind of loving conversation. The cinema reduced dialogue to the minimum: "Film-making," said Truffaut, "is pointing the camera at beautiful women." John Wayne's cowboy was essentially silent. In one film the heroine says to him, "You don't need anybody but yourself." He replies, "I want a woman who needs me." That's all he wants a woman to say. But when she adopts the tactic of putting on a sexy dress, he says, "You wear those things and I'll arrest you." She says, "I thought you were never going to say it." "Say what?" "That you love me." "I said I'll arrest you." "It means the same thing, you know that. You just won't say it."

For a time, Rhett Butler's method in *Gone with the Wind* of provoking affection by aggression, and proving his superiority by humiliating women, was a substitute for conversation. Then the shy, naive, simple male, who has to be coached by women to love, was developed. It became the woman's role to mend the man with problems and complexes. It was only rarely that people like Bogart added a bit of wit and repartee. Woody Allen is the exception. He loves not only to talk, but even to say what he's thinking while he's talking, as he does in the subtitles to *Annie Hall*. But his films are about incompetence. Since so many people feel incompetent, they can identify with him, but he doesn't help them. The cinema has provided models of only a few kinds of success, and has never known how to cope with quiet contentment, the happiness of fulfillment. What films can you recall which analyze a successful marriage? In the cinema, love is found by the meeting of the eyes much more than by talk, and it is essentially a chase. The cinema has not been able to get beyond Dostoyevsky's claim that happy people have no history. So how are people supposed

Unfair lovers

to know what to talk about in a good relationship?

In the theater, dialogue used to be refined and raised to its most powerful expression. Shakespeare showed how it could create passion and action. Ibsen revealed how people could be transformed by their dialogue. One of his characters says, "A change has come over me, and that change has come through you, through you alone." That is a strong justification of conversation. But since then, playwrights have been more obsessed by the difficulty of communicating. Beckett showed characters who want to talk, but can't say anything.

We have come to the end of a phase in culture. We no longer have the literature or art which can help us invent the kind of conversation we need if we are to move beyond the reiteration of our own helplessness and disarray. Depictions of despair, incoherence and violence make us more helpless still. For about a century now, we have been brought up to believe in the virtues of introspection. But asking that same old question, "Who am I?" cannot get us much further. However fascinating one may think one is, there is a limit to what one can know about oneself. Other people are infinitely more interesting, have infinitely more to say.

Particularly now that the great aspiration of the present generation is to give the sexes equal rights and equal respect. Conversation is the best way of creating the conditions for

Self-portraits

this: better than laws, because laws cannot change mentalities, and conversation can. There can be no satisfactory conversation without mutual respect. Respect discovers the equal dignity of others. Start with private life, and other forms of equality will eventually spread in public life.

So we need models of how conversations develop equality, models created by a joint effort of men and women. We know enormous amounts about how relationships go wrong. It is much harder to show how they go right, without arrogance or naiveté or the fear that once love is analyzed, it will lose its magic. We need a new kind of novel and film to create visions of how people can live together as equals, with humor. All previous civilizations have had models of virtuous living. They don't work for us, they seem amazingly boring. But there are an increasing number of people who are, privately, doing something very interesting, exciting, trying to give each other courage. They are doing something new, because this is the first time in history that men and women have been equally educated and doing the same jobs. Nothing is more difficult than to acquire self-confidence without arrogance. It is the basis of all worthwhile achievement. We need art to show how courage grows. And if famous artists are too tortured to know, then we need to do it without them, to realize that we too are artists, however humble, and that creating equal conversations is now the supreme art.

Our ancestors thought they could become brave by imitating brave heroes. We are too conscious of our frailties to do that, and have lapsed into identifying with antiheroes. I think the hero in our generation is not the individual but the pair, two people who together add up to more than they are apart. The most inspiring theater today takes place in our homes, when our improvised conversations can leave us feeling that humans are not just despicable creatures, but can be inspiring, brave, hopeful also. It sometimes happens, we wish it could happen more often. We need filmmakers to tell us how it can happen, without sentimentality, without complacency. Film could have a revolutionary effect on our conversation. For the first time in history, we can see ourselves as others see us.

Our private conversations do make a difference to the world. A relationship may start chemically or romantically, but conversation adds something infinitely precious to it. Having one's ideas challenged and transmuted by verbal intercourse makes one aware how much one owes to others, how much a partner can contribute to one's intellectual, moral and emotional development, though one remains a separate, unique person. It is in private that one can best

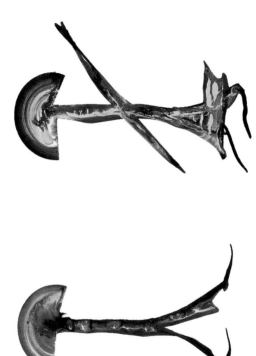

Conversation with someone who ate barbed wire for breakfast

learn how to accept criticism. Two individuals, conversing honestly, can be inspired by the feeling that they are engaged in a joint enterprise, aiming at inventing an art of living together which has not been tried before. Even wall-papering the house together can be more than a shared chore, more than a shared entertainment, particularly if one makes one's own wallpaper. In the process, one can change one's idea of beauty, and when that happens, one is changed oneself.

So how many engagements were broken off yesterday? I spoke to a woman the other day who had done just that. And I asked her about what had happened to her conversations. She valued them enormously. She liked to talk to her boyfriend exactly as she talked to her women friends. She spent a great deal of time talking to herself, thinking about all the things she would be doing, what she would be wearing, what she would be cooking. But one thing she did not think about was how she spoke. That, she said, came naturally. I don't agree. In my view, conversation deserves more thought than cosmetics.

The question you might ask is: Can conversation really change the kind of love we feel? You might argue that nice people who like each other will inevitably have nice conversations. But I would reply that mutual attraction has notoriously never been enough to produce free and easy relationships. Lovers are increasingly not satisfied with just being loved: they want to know why they are loved, and that involves conversations; compliments are not enough. Take the case of a woman I have met who, despite her beauty, has always had trouble with men, because she argues rather than converses: she feels she has to win her arguments to prove that she is the equal of her man, she is relentless until he gives in; the result is mutual exhaustion. Or take the case of another woman who is too uncertain about what she thinks, or about her ability to express herself, so that she leaves men constantly guessing about her feelings, and gives the impression of being colder than she is. In both cases, I don't think the answer is simply for them to explain what they feel, because so long as they feel it, the same results will follow. But in conversation feelings are handed back and forth until an intimacy develops, and the other person's concerns become one's own. Love ultimately means that another person's welfare, hopes and fears matter as much as one's own. Physical contact is the basic source of intimacy, but conversation extends that intimacy to many aspects of life where holding hands is not enough. That's why I think we are entering a new age in the conversation of love.

3

What saves family conversation from being boring

Here is a seventeen-year-old boy talking about conversation at home: "I feel patronized in every conversation with my parents. They think they're superior. They treat me at a low intellectual level. I have much better conversations with my friends. So I don't really put in the effort for a real conversation at home. Dad never really listens. Mom has to take center stage without being interrupted. I think it's legitimate to interrupt: it shows interest. It's better with my friends because they treat me as a peer, and they get impassioned about things, which parents don't. A conversation should be fueled by the passion that we have for the subject."

But this boy's mom says she's starved of conversation,

though she is a councilwoman, and a lawyer, and used to be a teacher, and has spent much of her life talking. "Without conversation," she says, "the human soul is bereft. It is almost as important as food, drink, love, exercise. It is one of the great human needs. If deprived of it, we die. People in solitary confinement, like Terry Waite, keep themselves sane by having imaginary conversations with themselves."

The sad fact, she says, is that what with constant interruptions and the phone ringing, there is not enough time in her busy life for real conversations, which she likes to be leisurely, relaxed, and with people sharing the talk equally. Her conversations, she says, have therefore become passive ones, watching television or listening to radio. "I really enjoy other people having conversations for me," she says. Because in her dinner parties her guests are too often, as she puts it, "egos shouting, 'Look at me! Aren't I great?' And none really want to hear what the others say." Her conclusion is that she is happier talking to strangers than people who already know her. They are more inclined to listen.

There is a myth that conversation was once the backbone of family life, before the age of snack foods, when there was nothing to do at home except talk. In fact, there were plenty of fathers who enjoyed terrifying their families into silence, or going out to the bar to talk to their buddies rather than

Family conversation

their wives and children. Family rebellion, jealousy and rivalry caused as much silence as television ever did. And even in traditional societies, where supposedly the family is strong, the range of conversation could be strictly limited. The film director Ang Lee makes one of his Taiwanese characters say: "We worry for each other, and that makes us a family." The Japanese film *Family Life* shows conversation in terminal decline, with the children having nothing to say to their parents. In Brazil, I met people who loved talking but who said their grandparents spent long periods saying very little. It is not the only country where traditionally dance and song have been the preferred way of expressing feelings which could not be mentioned in conversation.

If we want family conversation, we have to invent a new sort, suited to our times. We have to think more clearly about what families do. They are not just havens of peace, where you can shut yourself off from the hostile and complicated world, where you can relax and feel free. Every time a couple get married, they start a conversation between two families which may never have met. They bring together in-laws and cousins of different ages, possibly of different nationality or social class, who did not choose each other. The family is the greatest teacher of the art of talking to strangers. So family conversation can only flourish if the family is seen as a safe place to make discoveries about the world, and to discuss them, to digest them, without fear.

The family meal is central in this adventure. It is where we learn to talk in a civilized way, at least that's the ideal. But good talk at meals is a rarity, an art we still have to develop. Eating together was often almost a religious service, celebrating being together and belonging, but not necessarily involving talk. In Elizabethan England, foreign visitors commented on how meals were eaten in silence. There are Chinese and Indian etiquette books which say you should not talk at meals. The Italian ones add: "Talk is not for the table, but for the piazza." The ancient Greeks carefully separated dining from the symposium for entertainment afterward. An anthropologist reporting on an Indonesian city says, "I could not find a single family in my neighborhood who ate together. There was no dining room; each member of the family comes to collect a plate of food in his own time, and retires to eat it alone." Snacking is not a modern invention.

To have conversation at meals involves a special kind of hunger. The great French philosopher of gastronomy Brillat-Savarin made a distinction between the pleasures of eating and the pleasures of the table, the latter meaning convivial talk about subjects worth talking about. Shared

Child's talk

food can contribute a sense of well-being and friendliness, but also a great deal more. If you always serve exactly the same kind of food, you will soon run out of new things to say about it. More exotic cooking has expanded the conversation into other civilizations and other centuries. In the past, food stimulated rather awesome thoughts, conducive to silence. Each ingredient had magic qualities. Today, we are beginning to return to the notion that eating is participation in the processes of nature. Our meals are making us think about the callousness of our habits. Cooking has become part of the visual arts. Shopping for food is a game of hide-and-seek, with packagers concealing their secrets in small print. The time will come, I hope, when those who influence our ideas on food, the writers of newspaper articles about restaurants, and the makers of TV cooking shows, will begin to discuss the quality of the conversation which their delicious meals induce, and not concentrate only on the decor of restaurants, or the technicalities of recipes. We need to invent a new poetry of food, as our ancestors invented a language of flowers.

Many of the people who remember wonderful conversation at family meals suggest that it was because they regularly had guests of all kinds to turn their minds to new subjects. Conversation, like families, dies when it is

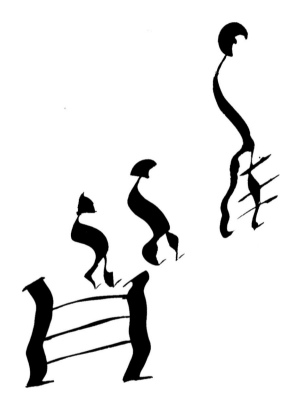

Family tradition

inbred. Or when your guests have had more or less the same experience as yourself. People of the same profession or with the same hobby have seldom produced the most inspiring talk when they have met. The family meal is made for stopping shop talk, and for mixing different kinds of talk. Conversation has to explore new territory to become an adventure.

In Jamaica, they have a system by which the locals invite foreign tourists for a meal, just for the pleasure of meeting strangers. We have lost this kind of family hospitality, which once existed all over the world, when, however poor, you would offer a free meal to any stranger passing by. "Be not forgetful to entertain strangers," says the Bible, "for thereby some have entertained angels unawares."

Family conversation has as its central but unstated theme how people of different temperaments and different ages can live together. For many centuries children were told to keep quiet. Some now get their revenge by dominating the meal; but they can contribute enormously to improving our capacity to understand other people. A professor of philosophy has published the text of his philosophical conversations with a class of elementary schoolchildren, to show that children are far more able and eager to think abstractly than adults generally recognize. Even a

Family friends

three-year-old was able to have this wonderful exchange, after watching his father eat a banana:

"You don't like bananas, do you Steve?" said the father.

"No," replied Steve. "If you were me you wouldn't like bananas either." After a pause for reflection, he added, "Then who would be the daddy?"

That's a good philosophical question. You could have a good conversation about that, particularly if we were taught how to think about such questions at school.

Children are given more encouragement in some countries than in others. Somebody who has studied children arguing while they play found that 31% of Italian children's disputes were about beliefs or opinions, but only 6% of American ones. Italian argument, apparently, is not only a dispute but also a display, a skillful performance produced by the enjoyment of conversation. American children had twice as many disputes about objects and play materials as Italian children, who emphasized style in their disputes, not just the need to win an argument, and who valued participation in a discussion above all else.

So the more we segregate children into a separate youth culture, the poorer our conversation, and theirs, will get. Perhaps it is time we gave them a more interesting role in the adult world and in family life.

The word from which "family" derives originally included not only kin but also servants. It extended to people of all classes, poor relatives, tutors, governesses, gardeners and cooks. A six-bedroomed manor house might have twenty servants. So people used to converse across class, though the conversation could be brutal and stressful. City planning has separated the rich and the poor. We have only recently begun to make a new start with conversation which ignores class differences, around common interests like sport or politics.

But talking to people with whom we apparently have nothing in common seems to me to be worth pursuing even further. This is what travel confronts us with: meeting people living a completely different life, with different traditions of conversation. I believe that humanity is a family which has hardly met. One of the best ways it can meet is for our traditions of family hospitality to be revived; that is where conversations with strangers can fruitfully begin.

So we need to take an interest in those traditions, and not to assume that ours is the only civilization which has struggled to improve conversation. For example, in ancient China there were women, organized in so-called poetry clubs, who met for conversation, discussing everything except the domestic chores they were supposed to be dedicated to. There have been Tamil women famous for their

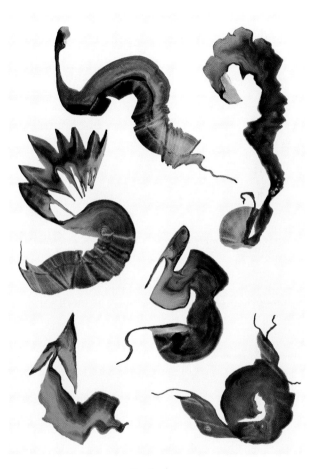

Family silence

conversation, and Arab women too, despite what has been written about the veil. There have always been exceptions, of individuals and couples, who have discovered how conversation can enrich life, and how destructive jealousy is. An ancient Chinese book on conversation is entitled: *The Soup That Cures Jealousy*.

So the family is shaped by the direction in which it points its conversation. It can focus on its memories and basically keep on saying, "This is the way we are, this is what the different members of the family have done and are doing." Or it may treat itself as a base from which its members set out to explore the outside world, and to which they return with something new to say, so that conversation is constantly enriched by outside as well as inside happenings. We become the prisoners of our families, our genes, our memories, only if we wish to be prisoners. It is by conversations with others, by mixing different voices with our own, that we can turn our individual life into an original work of art.

But what about those members of the family with whom we just cannot get on, who seem incorrigibly selfish or stupid? What about strangers who we think are wicked or whom we just don't like? I make a distinction between devils and horned devils. The horned ones enjoy being cruel, refuse to listen, and seem bent on destroying those around them, at least as independent beings. I hate to admit it, but there often is nothing you can do with them. I am far from claiming that we can cure all problems and automatically make nasty people nice. But most devils are not horned; they are aggressive because they are feeble, they are cruel because they are frightened. There is no need to give up on them. Families often find excuses for horned devils, and that can be a good thing as well as a bad thing. Families can stop people feeling completely deserted, and that is certainly worthwhile, because it is a necessary first step to seeing oneself as a human being.

The editor of the BBC's longest-running radio serial *The Archers* says that she tries to introduce ghastly people into the story for you to laugh at and say, "Aren't they awful?" But she finds that after a few months listeners begin to sympathize with them, the characters cease to appear quite so awful, and so the editor has to introduce new ghastly characters to replace them.

It is true that most people like to hate. Zola said, "Hate is holy." Hate makes people feel they have principles and opinions. But I would argue that finding something admirable, or touching, in an incomprehensible or obnoxious person, is also profoundly satisfying. The feelings of shared humanity, the tears which come to our eyes when we see suffering even

A room of one's own

in complete strangers, are among our deepest emotions. Every time we experience them, we are rediscovering that we belong to that enormous family which is humanity. Humanity means not just everybody, but also kindness. There are not many people totally devoid of some trace of kindness. To find that trace of gold, when it is hidden in apparently stony ground, is one of the most exciting of all challenges.

4

Conversation in the workplace:
why specialists are having to find
a new way of talking

It's up to us to decide on the kind of conversations we have. The way we talk at the office or factory shapes the work we do; it's not just machines which force us to be obedient. I want to show how we could make our work a lot less boring and frustrating if we learned to talk differently.

Look first at the case of the lawyer in the prosecutor's office who used to believe that he had a fascinating life dealing with criminals, but is now tired of listening to their lies, and even to their remorse. He's had enough of discussing the sordid side of life and of arguing with his bureaucratic colleagues. He can predict too accurately their words, their moves, their gestures. His job, he says, is not using all his intelligence. He wants to exercise his mind talking to more varied, more stimulating people, to discuss not just details but the big issues. He wants conversation which is more challenging and less routine. The legal profession is too stick-in-the-mud for him.

What advice would you give him? And what would you say to the financial wizard who was a brilliant mathematician in college and worked in insurance and stockbroking and became a millionaire, but then found, when he wanted to help the poor, that he had difficulty talking to them? He knew how to fix things, but he was not really comfortable in conversation with ordinary people. He didn't feel he could sympathize with them, as though after a lifetime in a job talking about money, his tongue would only move in one direction.

How much better off is he than the retired factory worker who remembers the days when it was impossible to speak in his workshop, because the noise was too deafening and the conversation consisted mainly of glances and gestures? He never really got to know his workmates well. They never found pleasure in talking about anything much except sports; he certainly never had a decent conversation with his boss. What has he missed?

What does work do to our conversation, and, in the process, what is it doing to us? Good conversation has become

Flowchart

a criterion of the quality of our private relationships; and now it is also taking a central place in our work.

Work increasingly consists of talk. In the old days, they used to have notices in factories saying, "Talk less. Work more." But today, try calling someone at the office, and they're always at a meeting. Go to a doctor's office, and watch how getting a diagnosis is now only a part of a medical consultation: doctors are expected to engage in a conversation between equals, in which the patient has as much right to question and demand as the doctor. In retailing, salespeople are trained not so much to obey orders as to talk to customers with a smile. Everywhere, the higher you climb up the hierarchy, the more time you spend discussing. There are very few pinnacles left where you need listen only to your own voice.

But the more we talk, the less there is that we can talk about with confidence. We have nearly all of us become experts, specialized in one activity. A professor of inorganic chemistry tells me that he can't understand what the professor of organic chemistry says. An economist openly admits that "Learning to be an economist is like learning a foreign language, in which you talk about a rational world which exists only in theory." The Princeton Institute of Advanced Studies, established to bring all the world's great minds together, was disappointed to discover that they did not converse much: Einstein, a colleague said, "didn't need anybody to talk to because nobody was interested in his stuff, and he wasn't interested in what anybody else was doing."

No wonder many young people hesitate to embark on highly specialized careers which make them almost feel they are entering prison cells. Indeed, one of Britain's major universities recently appointed the former head of the Prison Service to run its Careers Advisory Centre. An editor of *She* magazine has said, "We don't want to be defined by the job we do." An increasing proportion of those searching for a career feel they have talents which no single profession can nurture and develop. Even a producer I met in the corridors of the BBC in London, when I asked how his work was affecting his brain, said, "The job is narrowing my mind."

What job, then, offers the most enchanting and surprising conversations? Almost everyone says that the more varied the people they meet at work, the more fun it is, though often they exchange only a few words. But creativity usually needs to be fueled by more than polite chat. At the frontiers of knowledge, adventurous researchers have to be almost professional eavesdroppers, picking up ideas from the most unobvious sources. The discovery of DNA was the

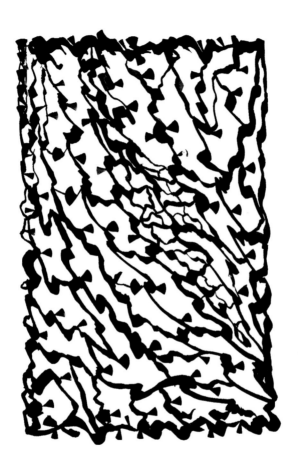

Team spirit

outcome of conversations between Crick and Watson, which went on ceaselessly for several years. They had only one rule, that they could say whatever came into their heads. Crick always preferred conversation to reading learned journals; he found it essential to meet the scientists who had done interesting experiments, because there would often be something unsaid in the colorless style which scientific papers adopt. He asked naive questions, insisting he had to simplify things for himself in order to understand them. That is how his conversations yielded new insights.

In the twenty-first century I look forward not to more modernity, or postmodernity, but to a sense of being part of a new conversation. My reason is the evidence I see everywhere of the ill-effects of specialization, valuable and necessary though that is. It needs to be balanced by its opposite. Some people may be happy to be a cog in a machine, but others have a different idea of what it means to be a human being. For them, the education and jobs on offer have become too narrow.

So I've been thinking about what kinds of work we might invent in the next century, and about what new kind of training that would involve, which does not just slot students into pigeonhole careers. I've talked to people in a vast range of occupations, and in nearly all of them it is clear that the best pleasures, the creative joys, are largely the privilege of a minority, and usually for brief periods. Nearly all of them complain that stress is increasing, and that drudgery has not been eliminated despite all our technology. Administrative chores are clogging our pores. Many professions, invented a long time ago, no longer command the respect they once did, or they incorporate outdated aspirations. Some have ethical problems, on the borderlines of dishonesty.

So let us ask what kind of human beings the new generation want to be, and see whether it is practical to invent jobs to suit them. Jobs to suit people, instead of making people behave in ways to suit the machinery or the institution. You may say that is impossible, that the young are being unrealistic in wanting jobs to enable them to enjoy everything that life can offer. I don't see it that way. The people of the Renaissance wanted variety too, and they often had more interesting lives than most of us do, as farmers, and diplomats, and engineers, and artists all at once.

Industry's leaders already realize that they must go in the Renaissance direction. Managers start as specialists, but as soon as they show signs of ability and get to the top, they become generalists, they have to understand the world as a whole, not just their specialty. But they are amateurs at

Anxieties in search of a home

being generalists: there is nowhere you can be trained to talk about everything, to be a Renaissance Person. Once upon a time, debutante girls were sent to finishing schools, to be able to make appropriate conversation in any situation. Modern managers have to be satisfied with being sent to business school, which does the opposite, concentrating their minds on increasing profits. In practice, the best managers move from industry to industry, but they have to concentrate on applying the same medicine to each one; and they are too overworked to reach the goal of the Renaissance Person. So something new is needed for students, managers and employees alike, for all those who sense that their mental processes are beginning to go rigid and want to make a last bid to remain free, who are not content to be just professionals, and who want jobs which will make them better people.

We have been inching toward this in voluntary service, hot-desking, multi-skilling, foundation courses, work experience, and an endless variety of short training courses, but without fundamentally changing the quality of conversation at work.

So I began thinking about how people who were not engineers or doctors or architects, or whatever, could have conversations with members of those professions, in which they would not feel complete outsiders. We admire actors because they know how to put themselves into the skin of another person. In our private lives, we are increasingly trying to see the world from the point of view of those we feel emotionally close to. It is time that in our work also we got rid of at least some of the barriers which prevent us from sharing the thoughts and language and style of other professions. The term "social exclusion" applies not only to the poor, but to all whose mind-set is confined to a single profession.

I asked a doctor how long it would take for her to teach me to be a doctor. "Six weeks," she said. Obviously, not to make me a real doctor, but to give me an idea of how doctors solve problems, of what a doctor's life does to the doctor. She was not guessing, because she had trained lay people in a poor country to assist her in her own medical practice, and after six weeks, they could do very useful work, under her supervision. After all, at least half of what one learns at college is promptly forgotten.

I asked an engineer how long it would take him to teach me to be an engineer. "Three months," he said. Not to be a real engineer, but to understand their language and their problems, to learn the essence of the way they think.

Would you be interested in the chance to spend time

The specialists

Downsizing

being initiated into three, four, even five different professions, learning to speak the language, experiencing the problems and the stresses, watching solutions being found, living in close proximity to those who make decisions, and seeing how many decisions are inevitable, and how many are arbitrary? I've had a small taste of this myself. A government minister once invited me to be his sort of shadow, accompanying him everywhere he went. It transformed my idea of what politics is about, what being a politician does to you.

I asked an architect, "Can I come and work in your office, without being a nuisance, to learn how the imagination of architects works?" I could be useful to him, he said. He would give me some drawings and get me to make a model of a building from them. The great problem for architects is to know in advance what an idea on paper will look like when it is built. Another person's visualization of his drawings would be helpful.

A series of such conversations, if carefully planned, could be an alternative to postgraduate training. Or they could be a part of management training. But the wider implication is that they would demystify the professions, giving outsiders a better understanding of the problems they face. They would provide the basis of experience needed to remodel the world of work, to create new combinations of professions. And they would give the prosecution lawyer and financier and factory worker I mentioned more opportunities to talk about their experience to the young. If one would rather have lived one's life differently, it is a consolation if one can prevent others from making the same mistakes.

You may object that the purpose of work is to make a profit, to ensure survival, that specialization is inescapable, that we should get our conversational pleasures in our leisure time. I would reply that the separation of life into work and leisure has had as many evil consequences as desirable ones. The truly privileged today are the small minority for whom work is pleasure. In the past, work was as much a social as an economic activity, often a family activity too. Go to an old-fashioned oriental bazaar, and you will find shopkeepers as interested in making friends with you, to the extent of offering you coffee, as in closing a sale. Modern managers consider them to be inefficient, which they may be commercially, but from the point of view of the shop-keeper's whole life, concerned with being integrated in a wider community than his own commercial one, it is very efficient.

The oriental bazaar is a reminder that humanity's evolution has not just been toward a consumer society, though

Human resources

abundance and prosperity for all is an almost universal goal. The other side of our evolution has been toward a service society, in which personal knowledge – almost intimacy with one's customers – is essential, as opposed to a consumer society, where you can buy anonymously without saying a word to the cashier. We now have to adjust our economic institutions to take more account of our desires.

The idea that we have reached the end of history once each of us has a profession, and are masters of its jargon, is absurd. Humans are no longer what they were when they invented the idea of the profession as a sort of secret society with a monopoly of knowledge. The more we see of the world, the broader is the range of our curiosity. At the moment, that broad curiosity is fanned more by the media than by universities or by work. We shall have to expand the conversation of both if we want to avoid being asphyxiated by them.

5

What technology can do to conversation

If you could invent a gadget, a piece of technology, which would really change your life, what would it be? I don't mean a gadget which would just make some little task more convenient, like a better corkscrew, but one which changed your personal life, your relationships, your ability to cope with the world. Well, you'd first of all have to think about what technology has done to private life in the past, what it's done to the way people talk.

For example, what has it done for a young woman who has tried a number of jobs over the last few years, none of which satisfied her, and who has now become a computer specialist? At last she's found an occupation where she can really concentrate, which she never could before. The machine demands her attention. She is proud that she can master it. But this new confidence is strictly limited.

Daisy chain

The computer has not radically improved her life outside her work. She has always been friendly, jolly, very kind, extraordinarily sensitive to other people's feelings. But unfortunately that makes her too worried about what people think about her. As soon as a conversation with a man becomes intimate, she gets scared. She is still too uncertain about herself, too conscious of her weaknesses, so that she is always frightened of being a fraud, of being found out, of being less than she appears to be. Computer technology has not so far transformed her as a person.

What more could it do? What more in particular could it do for people's private lives? Let's look first at what happened to conversation when the steam engine was invented, the great technological revolution which first transformed communications.

Trains divided the world into those who were frightened by them and those who talked lyrically about them as "the chariots of equality, freedom and civilization." The charismatic engineers who first proposed a Channel Tunnel in the 1850s were sure that, once a railway was built from London to Calcutta, all humanity would realize that it had common interests and war would be abolished. But many people were terrified by the noise and the new sensations caused by speedy travel, which transformed the shape of the landscape, almost like an earthquake. For example, the novelist Flaubert immediately hated trains. "I get so bored in them," he wrote, "I howl with tedium after five minutes. People think it's a dog. No. It's Monsieur Flaubert groaning." Flaubert was obsessed by boredom; and he found boredom almost everywhere he looked. His case is typical. Technology has repeatedly had the effect of accentuating existing attitudes, probably more than it has transformed them.

It was only those who wanted to be free and equal who found trains a place where they could enjoy the company of people they had never met before. The middle classes, who were bent on showing their superiority to the rabble, made the train a place where you cut yourself off from others who might be inferior, and with whom it might not appear respectable to associate. That is how second and first class cars became silent, devoted to reading newspapers and books. That is how railway newsstands first made their profits. It is very rare to find a well-to-do traveler complaining, as one did, that he envied those who traveled third and fourth class "from whose heavily populated carriages merry conversation and laughter rang all the way into the boredom of my isolation cell." In many poor countries today, you can still see vestiges of that division.

At a medical congress in 1866 a doctor said, "In the past,

The engineer's dream

whenever one knew that one was going to pass several hours, and sometimes several days, in the company of others, one tried to establish a rapport with one's companions, that often lasted beyond the duration of the journey. Today, we no longer think about anything but the impatiently-awaited and soon reached destination." And the sociologist Simmel wrote, "Before the development of buses, trains and streetcars in the nineteenth century, people were quite unable to look at each other for minutes or hours at a time . . . without talking to each other."

In the story of trains, you can see how the managers of technology collude in reinforcing tendencies which have nothing to do with technology. The railways had to decide what kind of cars they would build. The Europeans, following discussions between Britain and France, decided that passengers wished to be left alone while traveling. So the European compartment of about eight seats, unconnected to other compartments, was invented. By contrast, the Americans modeled their compartments on the steamboats, with big open spaces, allowing room to walk about. "An American", said a British journalist, "would not much care for our way of traveling in a fixed seat in a cramped carriage, under lock and key. He would sense a lack of air, of suffocation."

Eurostar is a new example of railway companies failing to think about what they are doing when they design new technology. Eurostar's cars assume that people wish to travel in twos or fours, and that most of them want to look at the backs of each other's heads. The designers could have said, "There are all sorts of travelers. Some want silence and some want to talk, just as some want to smoke and some don't. Some want to talk to people they know, and some want to make new friends. Some might want a host to introduce them, to treat them as individuals, rather than a guard blaring at them through loudspeakers, thanking them for choosing Eurostar. Some might want to learn languages while they waste three hours in a train." They could have made all sorts of different cars. But they did not. In other words, technology does not automatically improve conversation, communication, or behavior.

Now look at television. Commentators have concentrated on whether it has made us more violent, or illiterate, and accused it of destroying conversation. Again, what television has done, with some exceptions, is to reinforce existing prejudices. People have interpreted programs to suit their existing beliefs. Dallas, for example, was successful in 90 countries, but not in Brazil or Japan. Brazilian audiences rejected it because they have highly successful soap operas

Muzak

of their own, which have this originality, that the script is rewritten the day before they are transmitted, to contain references to current events, so that the serial becomes a commentary on everyday life, a part of everybody's conversation. The Japanese, for their part, quickly stopped watching *Dallas*, because they didn't want to change their preference for stories with happy endings. They found *Dallas* old-fashioned, because it was about conflict which remained unresolved, whereas for them, the purpose of a story of this type is to show how good relations can be reestablished. *Dallas*, they said, doesn't give us a dream. We want to go to bed happy.

Everywhere else that *Dallas* was watched, it did produce a lot of conversation. Arabs on the whole saw it as a challenge to their own values, and it made them reassert what they considered to be their opposing values. Sue Ellen, however provoked by her husband, should not have behaved the way she did. She should not have drunk or smoked. But they were fascinated by it as a family story, because kinship relations are one of their favorite subjects, so they discussed that side of the series. Russians used it to confirm their view that the rich were unhappy, that American civilization was rotten, that Americans had no culture – there was never a single scene of anybody reading a book – and some, imagining conspiracies everywhere, argued about whether there was a conspiracy by the producers of *Dallas* to make a serial which was secretly subversive of American institutions.

By contrast, most Americans seemed to think that *Dallas* had no message; it was just entertainment. Some talked about it in the same way as they talked about the weather, while others discussed it as TV connoisseurs, analyzing the form of the program and its technical construction.

So though *Dallas* did produce a lot of conversation, it didn't change opinions. It made no difference to the American audience who believed that the characters in it, like all people, were governed by irrational drives created by childhood events; it didn't change the Russians' view that people are formed by society; and it didn't change the Arabs' attitude that individuals are free to struggle against temptation, and that conversation should be about what is right and what is wrong.

Computer technology has already produced the same two kinds of talk that trains did. On the one hand are those who are euphoric about how it will end passive television watching and replace it with interactive conversation, with distance learning and international conviviality.

But, on the other hand, the world's poor cannot join in

Audience figures

the conversation: they have no computers and no telephones either, though they have waited over a century for them. Nor can the old join in, the computer illiterate, having less and less to talk about with the young, who will eventually perhaps refuse to pay their pensions. Computers vastly increase the control that management has over workers; every mistake can be recorded; pressures are being intensified. Computer technology in an office doesn't just mean that everyone can participate in the communal conversation on e-mail, but also that those competing for power can use it as a new weapon in their struggles against their rivals, and in their efforts to defend their territory.

Technology has not totally eliminated the tone of humility set by religion, which reigned unchallenged in the past, and which partly survives in the dread of terrible, apocalyptic catastrophes. But it has encouraged many people to talk as though there is a solution to every problem, and success is within everybody's grasp. So we have ended up divided as always between optimists and pessimists. I am interested in getting beyond that ancient argument, beyond thinking one has only two choices, either to be cynical or to be naive. The tone of conversation has a great influence on its content, and so on the agenda humans set for themselves.

The challenge now is to develop a new tone, and a new

kind of conversation, which is both hopeful and aware of the likelihood of failure. That tone can be inspired by the fact that the computer can allow people to speak and think more freely, despite the efforts of secretive governments; that it makes totalitarian controls ever harder to sustain; that it can give greater equality to the handicapped and the physically isolated; that it can enable families working in different parts of the world to preserve affections which would otherwise decay; that e-mail is creating a new kind of letter-writing culture, often between people who have never met. Technology can provide more opportunities to discuss how we can improve our lives, to tell others what our dreams are.

But where it can bring about a fundamental shift in our view of the future is by training us to cope with failure and to get beyond an over-simple expectation of success. So far, we have thought of technology in terms of gadgets which work. But it has now become obvious that all technology can have bad as well as good results, bring unexpected disasters as well as benefits. The time-saving car and the noisy, polluted, traffic-jammed city are obvious examples. Radio stations likewise: increasing our knowledge enormously, but failing to give coherence to our knowledge.

We have enough experience of technology now to be able to envisage bringing an end to the wasteful war between optimists and pessimists. Technology is not just concerned with making robots, to act predictably; humans will never behave predictably, and technology is no use to us from that point of view. It is also an endless series of experiments, many of which go wrong, and yet it never becomes discouraged, because just occasionally it discovers something really wonderful. If we saw our lives as a series of experiments, we would become less discouraged by our inevitable failures.

It's always assumed technology has a simple goal, basically to save effort, to economize, to make life more comfortable. But it also does something much more adventurous, potentially poetic, trying to bring about marriages between human intelligence and the mysteries of nature. Occasionally those marriages show quite marvelous intuition, as amazing as any we find in the world of the arts. So we should not say that working with things is so much simpler than working with people, that there is nothing to be learned from it from the point of view of our emotions, our depressions, or our anger.

When I asked you what gadget you would like to invent, it was out of genuine interest, because I have always been fascinated by gadgets, that is to say, by ingenuity. But increasingly I've become interested also in what lies behind invention, in the process by which new insights are

Baby alarm

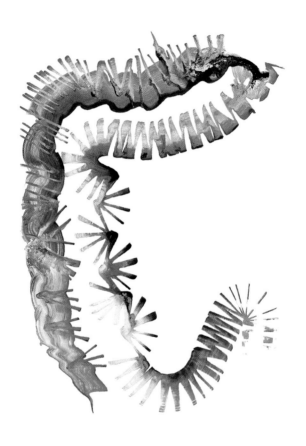

Digesting information

discovered. The really big scientific revolutions have been the invention not of some new machine, but of new ways of talking about things. How we talk about our private lives can change in revolutionary ways too. And the revolution we need today is in the way we talk about failure. The conclusion I draw from the history of technology is that it has managed to deal with failure on the whole more sensibly than we have dealt with failure in our political or private lives, perhaps because failure is regarded by engineers as their central problem. They know it is impossible to conceive an airplane which could not crash.

So technology can provide us with some useful models. We need to start using conversation to create courage in the face of failure, a balanced kind of courage, which can resist disappointment, and which can at last make us immune to the cynicism which has so long been our scourge.

6

*How conversation encourages
the meeting of minds*

One of the most silent men I have known ended up committing suicide. When I was an undergraduate, the philosophy tutor of my college used to organize lunches in his rooms, inviting three or four students from different subjects. He brought us together for conversation, but he hardly ever spoke himself. And yet there was a wonderful warmth radiating from him, a gentleness, a modesty, which somehow made us talk, shy and ignorant though we were. We felt we had to respond to his kindness. I remember those stunted conversations as among the most moving I have ever had. Then one day he left a note outside his door, warning visitors that he had turned on the gas and that they would find him dead. Nobody knows why. Perhaps he felt he could not reach the impossibly high standards he set for himself. But he knew how to bring people together. A conversation brings people and ideas together; and it's not disastrous if you keep silent while you watch ideas meeting.

"It's good to talk." I've said that this advertising slogan is a half-truth, but it is also revolutionary. For most of history, people have believed that silence was an ideal they should strive for, a mark of wisdom. We've moved from one extreme to another. We now feel like fools when we go to a party and can't think of anything to say. In the past that would not have been so awful. Today we should remember that tongue-tied people are often busy having conversations which are as valuable and as exciting as any other, conversations with themselves. That means thinking. Talk without thought is empty. Change the way you think, and you are halfway to changing the world.

I see thinking as bringing ideas together, as ideas flirting with each other, learning to dance and embrace. I appreciate that as a sensuous pleasure. Ideas are constantly swimming around in the brain, searching like sperms for the egg they can unite with to produce a new idea. The brain is full of lonely ideas, begging you to make some sense of them, to recognize them as interesting. The lazy brain just files them away in old pigeonholes, like a bureaucrat who wants an

The roundabout route

easy life. The lively brain picks and chooses and creates new works of art out of ideas.

The peculiarity of humans is that they can watch themselves as they go about their business, as they talk and think. They have, as it were, two internal voices, so they can both create new ideas and look at them, criticize or admire. They can be either slaves of their thoughts and memories, or decide which of them are useful, which cause only trouble, and which to put away in a bottom drawer. Conversation with yourself is full of risk, because you have to decide how much to enhance your ideas with imagination. The really deprived are those who say they have no imagination, or no sense of humor, which is almost the same thing. Dostoyevsky claimed that it doesn't matter what people say, only how they laugh. It's true that you cannot be free or fully human until you laugh, because to laugh means to make your own judgment, to refuse to accept things at their face value, but also not to take yourself too seriously. That means inviting other people to your internal conversations and discovering that they see you quite differently from the way you see yourself.

Jane Austen said that you cannot make good conversation if you read only newspapers, implying that only books contain enough stimulating ideas to enable you to turn topical issues into discussions of a general kind. That, of course, depends on whether the newspaper contains only tidbits of disconnected news. I agree that a conversation cannot just consist of anecdotes, because you have to tie the anecdotes together with a general thought which can then be discussed. Ideas need not just to meet, but to embrace.

One average-sized book would take about twelve hours to read out on the radio. Radio can do many of the things that books do, and has other advantages (you can wash up or garden at the same time as listening), but it will not replace books until you can say to a radio, "Stop, wait a minute, please repeat that, give me time to think about it." If I were to pause for more than a second when talking on the radio, the station manager would think something was wrong. Conversation needs pauses, thoughts need time to make love.

I particularly value conversations which are meetings on the borderline of what I understand and what I don't, with people who are different from myself. For most of history, what people have disagreed most about is religion, which was the topic of a very large proportion of conversations in the western world until about two centuries ago. I like conversations which discover that people with apparently differing standpoints can reach a meeting of minds on some subjects, limited though they might be. Since religion still

The gate of understanding

continues to dominate discussion in many parts of the world, bringing believers and unbelievers together in conversation seems urgent as well as interesting.

For example, many people say that they have conversations with God. These have had an enormous influence on behavior throughout history, either by spurring bold action, or by providing consolation for misfortune. The conversations of mystics could provide a good starting point for discussions of the art of detachment, of not being overwhelmed by human suffering, which many people attempt today without any religious thought. The Persian Ansari, for example, who lived in the eleventh century and whose book *Intimate Conversations* remained popular for centuries, talked like this to God: "When I look upon You, I see myself a king among kings, a crown on my head. When I look upon myself, I see myself among the humble, dust on my head. There is no joy without pain from You. There is no freedom except in bondage to You." There is much to discuss in that.

Contrast Ansari with a modern American woman who has written down her conversations with God, not in fine poetry, but in a way that could lead to quite different thoughts. She said to God: "When I peel potatoes, I feel near you. I'm so sick of housework, sick of the children. They get on my nerves, so I could scream. (And do.) I'm even sick of my husband at the moment. I wish he'd go away on a business trip. Maybe my husband feels trapped too. Lord, help me to realize how lucky I am here – within this tender trap. Turn my fantasies of escape to some useful purpose. Bless that person you surely want me to be, instead of a self-pitying drudge. Keep me at it." At a time when perhaps as many people are moving toward religion as are moving away from it, and when many are becoming fundamentalists, it is important to converse with them, to understand what thoughts lie behind their religious dedication.

Bringing people of different nations together for sport and music is useful and fun, but only long conversations can reveal the full meaning of the deep resentment felt by many civilizations toward the West. What we consider to be our triumphs – our freedoms, our empire or our technology – are viewed quite differently by them. Never has there been more need for conversation between civilizations, because never have they been able to inflict so much damage on each other. Our sensibilities are gradually changing, as more and more westerners visit India, for example, and discover what bitter memories the British Raj has left, even among people who can quote British poets to us better than we can remember them ourselves. The conversation between civilizations is being transformed by the new modesty which is entering

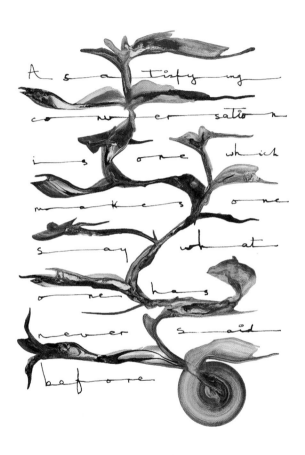

A satisfying conversation is one which makes one say what has never said before

The scribe's contribution

our historical memories. We remember that India five hundred years ago was the richest country in the world. The more we meet different forms of gentleness and conviviality, even in misfortune, the less we can boast about our victories, the less we can be satisfied with the bitterness of so much of our own conversation. When we watch Indian dance, for example, which is a breathtakingly beautiful alternative to verbal conversation, we realize how much we still have to learn in the art of communication.

Our sensibilities also change when we visit the Islamic world, which at the beginning of the second millennium was the most splendid of all civilizations of the time, and when we converse with Islamic women, to discover the enormous variety of conditions they experience, in different countries, in different classes, to realize how their position has changed many times in the course of history, and how it is changing now, when we appreciate that Islam has been interpreted in ways as varied as Christianity or any other religion. God says in the Koran, "We have created you male and female and made you nations and tribes, *that you may know one another.*"

Conversation puts you face to face with individuals, and all their human complexity. Our education cannot be complete until we have had conversations with every continent, and every civilization. It is a humbling experience, which makes one conscious of the enormous difficulty of living in peace when there is so much injustice, but which also gives one great hopes, every time one succeeds in having a conversation which establishes a sense of common humanity, a mutual respect. After such conversations, one can never be the same person again.

You may wonder whether the art of conversation should be taught, or can be taught, like dancing. The Victorians thought so. They poured out a vast mass of books on the subject, showing that they felt a new style was needed for their new ambitions. But the conversation they wanted to learn had aims which would not entirely satisfy the present generation: to make time pass more agreeably, to get the good opinion of others and to improve oneself. The teachers of conversation neglected the idea of personal contact, of the intimate meeting of minds and sympathies and, above all, of the search for what life is about, and how we should behave. They assumed everybody knew what life was about. They regarded themselves as propagating a branch of knowledge between music and medicine; that is, they became elocutionists, correcting accents and presentation, instead of deepening the subject matter of conversation. For most of history, people aspiring to be conversationalists

I didn't catch that

Maturity

have too often avoided subjects which went too deep or were too personal. They cheated: instead of saying what they thought, they repeated fashionable formulae or found epigrammatic ways of saying things they did not believe.

I hope the new century will be more adventurous. Mere personal advancement or respectability can no longer be the main purpose of conversation. What is missing from the world is a sense of direction, because we are overwhelmed by the conflicts which surround us, as though we are marching through a jungle which never ends. I should like some of us to start conversations to dispel that darkness, using them to create equality, to give ourselves courage, to open ourselves to strangers, and most practically, to remake our working world, so that we are no longer isolated by our jargon or our professional boredom. We cannot reproduce the Renaissance; history cannot be made to repeat itself; but we can create something akin to it, to suit ourselves.

That is what I call the New Conversation.

One final word. This is the last of my six talks, but for me they have not been just talks. They are part of a larger project I'm engaged in, to actually try to make a change in the way life is lived. I have received many letters from people in many countries who have read my books, and who say that what I have written echoes their own experiences and aspirations.

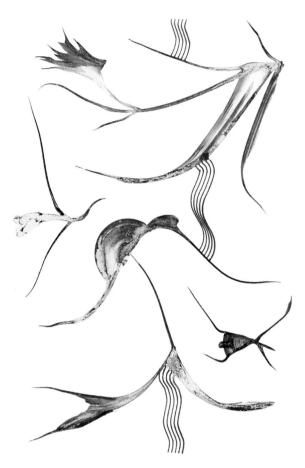

Thinking for oneself

They confirm me in my belief that a new kind of group is growing up in the world, an affinity of people living in every continent, for whom the broadening of their curiosity is a major passion, and for whom travel abroad is an essential part of education, which is never complete. Already, 400 million people travel each year to another continent. I see an affinity of those who are impatient with the slow pace of change in public life, and who, while waiting for politics to increase the amount of justice – which may take centuries – believe that ordinary people can make big changes by improving the way they relate to each other in daily life. I personally think we ought to start on that adventure by helping young people to escape from the narrowness of specialist jobs and specialist training, to become generalists, and by giving older people more opportunities to share their experience with the young, to counter the segregation of the generations and of knowledge. I would be really glad if you were to tell me what you think.

Thirty-six topics of conversation

Chapter 1

1. *First words*
   What alternatives are there to the platitudes normally used to start a conversation?

2. *Copycats*
   How useful is it to imitate the conversational styles of others?

3. *The gate between the public and the private*
   Can good conversation be impersonal?

4. *Emotional wavelengths*
   How does one improve one's skill at guessing what people do not actually say?

5. *A cruel word*
   Is wit worth the price its victims pay?

6. *The wasted meeting*
   How can shy people be helped to talk?

Chapter 2

7. *The signals of love*
   Why do lovers so often say that they cannot express their love in words?

8. *First impressions*
   Why do we talk of love at first sight, but seldom of love at first sound?

Chapter 4

19. *Flowchart*
    Is a successful conversation one which goes exactly as planned?

20. *Team spirit*
    What place is there in conversation for the competitive instinct?

21. *Anxieties in search of a home*
    Are you in the wrong job if you cannot share your personal worries with your colleagues?

22. *The specialists*
    Can you tell from the way someone talks what their work is?

23. *Downsizing*
    What is the antidote for conversations which make one feel small?

24. *Human resources*
    Is it possible to have a conversation with a customer, if the customer is always right?

Chapter 5

25. *Daisy chain*
    How could a technical education enhance poetic sensibilities?

26. *The engineer's dream*
    Is the most worthwhile conversation one which takes most risks?

27. *Muzak*
    How do the sounds which surround us influence the way we think and talk?

28. *Audience figures*
   How much do you rely for your topics of conversation on the suggestions of the media?

29. *Baby alarm*
   What is the effect of electronic toys on conversation?

30. *Digesting information*

   Is it true that too much information gives you Irritable Owl Syndrome?

Chapter 6

31. *The roundabout route*
   When is digression necessary?

32. *The gate of understanding*
   In conversations between civilizations, is it more fruitful to discuss similarities or differences?

33. *The scribe's contribution*
   What can a letter do that a conversation cannot?

34. *I didn't catch that*
   Is it ever worth pretending to understand when you don't?

35. *Maturity*
   Do you like to have your opinion changed by conversation?

36. *Thinking for oneself*
   What kind of space, or time, is best for conversations with oneself?

Acknowledgments

I should like to thank BBC Radio 4 (and particularly Philip Sellars), who invited me to give these talks, reprinted here as they were spoken, with minimal changes. I am deeply grateful also, for help and kindness, to my friends Mark Garcia, Danielle Olsen, Corinna Gannon, Louise Allen, Christina Hardyment, Gideon Koppel, Georgina Vestey, Amarjit Barn, Mark Elvin, Tapan Raychaudhuri, Andrew Nurnberg, Christopher MacLehose and the members of The Harvill Press; to all those who have conversed with me or written to me and taught me what varied shapes conversation can take; and, above all, as always, to Deirdre.